D1288663

ALL KINDS OF LEGS

Solveig Paulson Russell

Illustrated by Bill Heckler

THE **BOBBS-MERRILL** COMPANY, INC.
A SUBSIDIARY OF HOWARD W. SAMS & CO., INC.
Publishers • INDIANAPOLIS • NEW YORK

Library of Congress Catalog Card No. 63-19002
Copyright © 1963 by Solveig Paulson Russell
Printed in the United States of America
First Printing

Some legs are short,
Some legs are long,
Some legs are weak,
And some are strong.
They come in pairs
Of two or more,
With many creatures
Having four.
But every leg
Has work to do,
And each leg is
Important, too.

Animals that have two legs are called *bipeds*. People have two legs, so people are *bipeds*.

With two legs people can walk, run, hop, and jump. People use their legs to run machines, to travel, to swim and to have fun.

Because people are the wisest of all animals they can use their legs in the greatest number of ways.

What can you do with your legs?

Birds have two legs.

Their feet often have claws so that they can hold onto limbs or scratch for food.

Some birds have long legs. Some birds have short legs.

Birds fold their legs against their bodies when they fly.

When songbirds sleep they perch on a limb. Then their legs fold neatly under them.

Their toes lock tightly on the limb so the birds will not fall off while they sleep.

A chicken scratches the dirt with its feet to find food.

It walks slowly, raising one foot at a time. Up, down! Up, down!

Chickens have sharp spurs on their legs. They sometimes use the spurs to fight.

A robin has two thin, strong legs.

He hops and runs on his legs. He skitters over the ground.

He spends much of his time on the ground, looking for worms, bugs, and seeds to eat. He needs running, hopping legs to find his food.

Sometimes he scratches his head with his foot.

Some birds who live near water have very long legs.
A crane has long legs.
A stork has long legs.
Long legs are good for wading birds. They keep the
bird's body out of the water while he searches the water
for food.

Some birds swim. Their legs have webbed feet. Webbed feet are good for swimming. Birds can push themselves forward in the water with their webbed feet. Swans, ducks, and geese have webbed feet.

The ostrich is the largest of all birds. It cannot fly, but it can run very fast. An ostrich can run as fast as a horse.

It has long, strong legs. Its toes have pads on them so it can run more easily in the sandy country in which it lives.

It uses its legs to kick, too.

Animals with four legs are called *quadrupeds*.

Many animals have four legs. Four legs make a sturdy support for large bodies.

Horses have four legs.

Cows have four legs.

Some animals with four legs can climb. Did you know that a bear can climb a tree? He can.

A raccoon can climb, too.

Animals that climb have strong claws to help them hold onto trees.

Some animals climb trees for protection. Some climb for the food they find in tree bark and branches.

Some animals, like the frisky squirrels, make their homes in trees.

Squirrels have four legs, so they are *quadrupeds*. Their front legs are short and their back legs are long.

A squirrel can hold nuts with its front claws.

A squirrel's strong back legs help it sit up and jump from tree to tree.

Squirrels can climb easily. They have sharp claws to hold onto trees.

A mole has four legs. It has big front feet with sharp claws on them. A mole uses its strong front legs to dig tunnels in the earth so that it can find worms and bugs to eat. Moles live in the ground.

Frogs can live in water and on dry land.

Their short front legs support their heads and shoulders.

Frogs have strong, long back legs. Frogs jump with their strong back legs. They help frogs dive into the water, KERSPLASH! They give them a big push when they want to move fast. They help them swim.

A turtle has four stubby legs and a hard shell on its back.

A turtle can pull its legs and head into its shell when it feels danger is near. Then it just looks like a shell, with no legs at all.

Many hundreds of years ago seals lived only on land. Then they had feet at the end of their legs. But when seals began to live in water their feet gradually turned into flippers.

On land seals push themselves forward with their flippers. They can spring quickly on their strong back flippers.

In the ocean they use their flippers to swim.

A sloth is an animal with four legs. But it does not use them for walking. It lives its life hanging from trees.

Its toes have claws which are so big and curved that it cannot walk easily. The claws are made to fit around tree limbs, for a sloth uses its legs and claws to hang upside down from trees. It moves along tree limbs slowly as it eats young leaves and tender buds.

Bats are four-legged animals that fly.

Bats' legs are not strong because they do not use their legs often.

Their wings are made of skin which grows from their front legs to their back legs.

Bats fly at night.

They sleep during the day by hanging upside down in dark places.

Beavers live in lakes and streams and are very good swimmers.

They use their front legs to build homes and dams. They use them to dig ditches so they can float logs to their dams. They use their legs to push sticks and mud where they want them.

Beavers have webbed feet on their back legs to help them swim.

Kangaroos have two short front legs and two big strong back legs.

Kangaroos use their two front legs like hands.

Kangaroos hop with their strong back legs and they sit up on them. They can hop fast and high. With their strong legs kangaroos can jump right over large bushes when they are frightened.

Giraffes have four very long legs.

They make a giraffe so tall that it can eat leaves from treetops.

A giraffe uses its long legs to run away from danger and to kick when it needs to fight.

A camel has four long, strong legs.

There are pads on the bottom of a camel's feet. The pads help keep the camel from sinking into the sand. Because camels can walk in sand, they are important in desert lands. Camels carry heavy loads across the deserts.

Elephants have four big strong legs, which are as heavy and round as tree trunks.

Elephants are very big animals. They need big strong legs to hold them up when they stand or walk.

Animals that have six legs are called *hexapods*.

All insects have six legs. Sometimes insects' legs are short. Sometimes insects' legs are long.

Insects' legs always bend easily so that they can crawl over the earth or plants.

A grasshopper has six legs.

Its back legs are very long and strong. They are jumping legs.

A grasshopper uses its back legs to hop and jump. Hopping is its way of moving quickly when danger is near. It hops from one blade of grass to another. That is why it is called a grasshopper.

Ants have six jointed legs with two tiny claws at the ends. They use the claws to help them hold onto the thing they want to move.

Ants can carry loads that are many times heavier than they are themselves.

Have you ever seen ants using their legs to carry food to their nest?

Spiders are not insects because they do not have six legs.

Spiders have eight legs. Their legs are as thin as thread.

Spiders use their legs to walk and to help them make webs. Spiders catch flies and other insects in their webs. Spider webs are nets to catch spider food.

Crabs have ten legs.

Their two front legs are long and strong. They have claws on them. The claws are used to catch and crush their food.

The rest of a crab's legs help it to walk.

All of a crab's legs have joints so that it can crawl over the ocean floor.

A centipede looks like a long worm with legs.
Some centipedes have more than a hundred legs. They
use their legs to move their long bodies. Two or four or
six legs would not be enough to move such a long body.

Legs, legs, everywhere,
On the ground and in the air.
Some small as pins,
Some large as trees,
Some straight as sticks
And some with knees.
Although they're often
Strange to see,
Legs are useful
As can be.